MONOLOGUES
FROM
THE CLASSICS
Roger Karshner, editor

Dramaline Publications
10470 Riverside, Drive, Suite #201
Toluca Lake, CA 91602
818/985-9148
Fax: 818/985-0408

On the cover: Sir Henry Irving

This book is printed on 55# Glatfelter acid-free paper, a paper that meets the requirements of the American Standard of Permanence of paper for printed library material.

CONTENTS

WOMEN/COMIC

The Merry Wives of Windsor,
William Shakespeare

Act II, i. Sir John Falstaff, a roué and profligate, has typically exercised indiscretion by sending a presumptuous love letter to Mistress Page who is outraged at his boldness.

MISTRESS PAGE

(*Enter Mistress Page, with a letter.*)

What, have I scap'd love letters in the holiday time of my beauty, and am I now a subject for them? Let me see.

(*She reads.*)

"Ask me no reason why I love you; for though Love use Reason for his physician, he admits him not for his counsellor. You are not young, nor am I. Go to then, there's sympathy. You are merry, so am I. Ha, ha! then there's more sympathy. You love sack, and so do I. Would you desire better sympathy? Let it suffice thee, Mistress Page—at the least, if the love of soldier can suffice—that I love thee. It will not say, pity me,—'tis not a soldier-like phrase; but I say, love me. By me,

> Thine own true knight,
> By day or night,
> Or any kind of light,
> With all his might
> For thee to fight.
>
> *John Falstaff.*"

1

What a Herod of Jewry is this! O wicked, wicked world! One that is well-nigh worn to pieces with age to show himself a young gallant! What unweighed behaviour hath this Flemish drunkard pick'd—with the devil's name!—out of my conversation, that he dares in this manner assay me? Why, he has not been thrice in my company! What should I say to him? I was then frugal of my mirth. Heaven forgive me! Why, I'll exhibit a bill in the parliament for the putting down of men! How shall I be reveng'd on him? For reveng'd I'll be, as sure as his guts are made of puddings.

The Taming of the Shrew, William Shakespeare

Act V, ii. Katherina has been conquered by Petruchio. An act which has resulted in a radical behavioral alteration. In this speech she expresses her new views relative to a woman's role of subservient femininity.

KATHERINA

Fie, fie! unknit that threat'ning unkind brow;

And dart not scornful glances from those eyes,

To wound thy lord, thy king, thy governor;

It blots thy beauty as frosts do bite the meads,

Confounds thy fame as whirlwinds shake fair buds,

And in no sense is meet or amiable,

A woman mov'd is like a fountain troubled,

Muddy, ill-seeming, thick, bereft of beauty;

And while it is so, none so dry or thirsty

Will deign to sip or touch one drop of it.

Thy husband is thy lord, thy life, thy keeper,

Thy head, thy sovereign; one that cares for thee,

And for thy maintenance commits his body

To painful labour both by sea and land,

To watch the night in storms, the day in cold,

Whilst thou li'st warm at home, secure and safe;

And craves no other tribute at thy hands

But love, fair looks, and true obedience;

Too little payment for so great a debt.

3

Such duty as the subject owes the prince
Even such a woman oweth to her husband;
And when she is froward, peevish, sullen, sour,
And not obedient to his honest will,
what is she but a foul contending rebel,
Amd graceless traitor to her loving lord?
I am asham'd that women are so simple
To offer war where they should kneel for peace;
Or seek for rule, supremacy, and sway,
When they are bound to serve, love, and obey.
Why are our bodies soft and weak and smooth,
Unapt to toil and trouble in the world,
But that our soft conditions and our hearts
Should well agree with our external parts?
Come, come, you forward and unable worms!
My mind hath been as big as one of yours,
My heart as great, my reason haply more,
To bandy word for word and frown for frown;
But now I see our lances are but straws,
Our strength as weak, our weakness past compare,
That seeming to me most which we indeed least are.
Then vail your stomachs, for it is no boot,
And place your hands below your husband's foot:
In token of which duty, if he please,
My hand is ready, may it do him ease.

The Beaux' Strategem, George Farquhar

Act II. Mrs. Sullen expresses negative views of marriage based on personal experience.

MRS. SULLEN

O Sister, Sister! If ever you marry, beware of a sullen, silent Sot, one that's always musing, but never thinks:—There's some Diversion in a talking Blockhead; and since a Woman must wear Chains, I wou'd have the Pleasure of hearing 'em rattle a little. —Now you shall see, but take this by the way—He came home this Morning at his usual Hour of Four, waken'd me out of a sweet Dream of something else, by tumbling over the Tea-table, which he broke all to pieces, after his Man and he had rowl'd about the Room like sick Passengers in a Storm, he comes flounce into Bed, dead as a Salmon into a Fishmonger's Basket; his Feet cold as Ice, his Breath hot as a Furnace, and his hands and his Face as greasy as his Flannel Nightcap.—Oh Matrimony!— He tosses up the Clothes with a barbarous swing over his Shoulders, disorders the whole Economy of my Bed, leaves me half naked, and my whole Night's Comfort is the tuneable Serenade of that wakeful Nightingale, his Nose.—Oh the Pleasure of counting the melancholy Clock by a snoring Husband!—But now, Sister, you shall see how handsomely, being a well-bred Man, he will beg my Pardon.

The Country Wife, William Wycherley

Act IV, ii. Mr. Pinchwife has dictated to his wife a letter of bitter outrage to Horner, a womanizer who goes about his love-debauchery with gleeful callousness. But Mrs. Pinchwife, disenchanted with her elderly husband and his need for jealous vengence, determines to pen her own letter, a letter of a flattering, "purple" nature which reveals her artfulness, resentments, and smoldering desires.

MRS. PINCHWIFE

"For Mr. Horner." So, I am glad he has told me his name. Dear Mr. Horner! But why should I send thee such a letter that will vex thee, and make thee angry with me? Well, I will not send it. Ay, but then my husband will kill me—for I see plainly that he won't let me love Mr. Horner—but what care I for my husband? I won't, so I won't, send poor Mr. Horner such a letter. But then my husband—but oh, what if I writ at bottom my husband made me write it? Ay, but then my husband would see't.—Can one have no shift? Ah, a London woman would have had a hundred presently. Stay—what if I should write a letter, and then wrap it up like this, and write upon't too? Ay, but then my husband would see't.—I don't know what to do.—But yet evads I try, so I will— for I will not send this letter to poor Mr. Horner, come what will on't.

"Dear, sweet Mr. Horner."

(*As she writes she reads what she has written.*)

So. "My husband would have me send you a base, rude, unmannerly letter; but I won't." So. "And would have me forbid you loving me; but I won't." So. "And would have me say to you, I hate you, poor Mr. Horner; but I won't tell a lie for him." There. "For I'm sure if you and I were in the country at cards together—" So. "I could not help treading on your toe under the table—" So. "or rubbing knees with you, and staring in your face, till you saw me." Very well. "And then looking down, and blushing for an hour together." So. "But I must make haste before my husband comes; and now he has taught me to write letters, you shall have longer ones from me, who am, dear, dear, poor, dear Mr. Horner, your most humble friend and servant to command till death.—*Margery Pinchwife.*"

Stay, I must give him a hint at bottom—so—now wrap it up just like t'other—so—now write, "For Mr. Horner." But oh now what shall I do with it? for here comes my husband.

The Provok'd Wife, John Vanburgh

Act I. Lady Brute has never truly loved her husband but she has remained a faithful and accommodating wife. But now, due to Sir John's indifference, she entertains the idea of philandering. In the following she justifies these thoughts.

LADY BRUTE

The Devil's in the Fellow I think. I was told before I married him, that thus 'twou'd be. But I thought I had Charms enough to govern him; and that there was an Estate. A woman must needs be happy; so my Vanity has deceived me, and my Ambition has made me uneasy. But some comfort still; if one would be reveng'd of him, these are good times; a Woman may have a Gallant, and a separate maintenance too—the surly Puppy—yet he's a Fool for't: For hitherto he has been no Monster: But who knows how far he may provoke me? I never lov'd him, yet I have been ever true to him; and that, in spite of all the attacks of Art and Nature upon a poor weak Woman's heart, in favour of a Tempting Lover.

Methinks so Noble a Defence as I have made, shou'd be rewarded with a better usage.—Or who can tell?—Perhaps a good part of what I suffer from my Husband may be a Judgement upon me for my cruelty to my lover.—Lord, with what pleasure could I indulge that thought, were there but a possibility of finding Arguments to make it good.—And how do I know but there may.—Let me see.—What opposes?—My

Matrimonial Vow?—Why, what did I Vow? I think I promis'd to be true to my Husband.

Well; and he promis'd to be kind to me.
But he han't kept his Word—

Why then, I'm so absolv'd from mine—ay, that seems clear to me. The Argument's good between the King and the People, why not between the Husband and the Wife? O, but that Condition was not exprest.—No matter, 'twas understood.

Well, by all I see, if I argue the matter a little longer with my self, I shan't find so many Bugbears in the way, as I thought I shou'd: Lord, what fine notions of Virtue do we women take up upon Credit of old foolish Philosophers. Virtue's its own reward, Virtue's this, Virtue's that;—Virtue's an Ass, and a Gallant's worth forty on't.

A Midsummer-Night's Dream, William Shakespeare

Act III, ii. Lysander and Demetrius, due to an error on the part of Puck, have fallen in love with Helena who believes them to be mocking her with their affections. Hurt and frustrated she admonishes them for such cruel sport.

HELENA

O spite! O hell! I see you all are bent

To set against me for your merriment:

If you were civil and knew courtesy,

You would not do me thus much injury.

Can you not hate me, as I know you do,

But you must join in souls to mock me too?

If you were men, as men you are in show,

You would not use a gentle lady so;

To vow, and swear, and superpraise my parts,

When I am sure you hate me with your hearts.

You are rivals, and love Hermia;

And now both rivals, to mock Helena:

A trim exploit, a manly enterprise,

To conjure tears up in a poor maid's eyes

With your derision! None of noble sort

Would so offend a virgin, and extort

A poor soul's patience, all to make your sport.

As You Like It, William Shakespeare

Act III, ii. Orlando is infatuated with Rosalind who is living a duplicitous existence. Here, as a man, she offers to cure Orlando by becoming his mistress and practicing irritants guaranteed to break him of his passion for Rosalind.

ROSALIND

Yes, [I once cured a man] and in this manner. He was to imagine me his love, his mistress; and I set him every day to woo me: at which time would I, being but a moonish youth, grieve, be effeminate, changeable, longing and liking, proud, fantastical, apish, shallow, inconstant, full of tears, full of smiles; for every passion something and for no passion truly anything, as boys and women are for the most part cattle of this colour; would now like him, now loathe him; then entertain him; then forswear him; now weep for him, then spit at him, that I drave my suitor from his mad humour of love to a living humour of madness; which was, to forswear the full stream of the world and to live in a nook merely monastic. And thus I cured him; and this way will I take upon me to wash your liver as clean as a sound sheep's heart, that there shall not be one spot of love in't.

As You Like It, William Shakespeare

Act III, v. As a means of survival Rosalind has disguised herself as a man and has set out to seek her father. During her quest she encounters Phoebe, a shepherdess who has wretchedly mistreated the shepherd Silvis. Outraged, Rosalind vilifies the shepherdess who, ironically, gives her heart to this "man."

ROSALIND

(Advancing.)

Who might be your mother,

That you insult, exult, and all at once,

Over the wretched? What though you have no beauty,—

As, by my faith, I see no more in you

Than without candle my go dark to bed,—

Must you be therefore proud and pitiless?

Why, what means this? Why do you look on me?

I see no more in you than in the ordinary

Of nature's sale-work. 'Od's my little life,

I think she means to tangle my eyes too!

No, faith, proud mistress, hope not after it:

'Tis not your inky brows, you black silk hair,

Your bugle eyeballs, nor your cheek of cream,

That can entame my spirits to your worship.—

You foolish shepherd, wherefore do you follow her,

Like foggy south puffing with wind and rain?

You are a thousand times a properer man

Than she a woman: 'tis such fools as you

That makes the world full of ill-favour'd children;
'Tis not her glass, but you, that flatters her;
And out of you she sees herself more proper
Than any of her lineaments can show her.—
But, mistress, know yourself: down on your knees,
And thank heaven, fasting, for a good man's love:
For I must tell you friendly in your ear,
Sell when you can: you are not for all markets:
Cry the man mercy; love him; take his offer:
Foul is most foul, being foul to be a scoffer.
So take her to thee, shepherd: fare you well.

WOMEN/DRAMATIC

The Winter's Tale, William Shakespeare

Act III, ii. Hermione defends herself in a court of law against charges of adultry.

HERMIONE

Since what I am to say must be but that
Which contradicts my accusation, and
The testimony on my part no other
But that comes from myself, it shall scarce boot me
To say "Not guilty." Mine integrity,
Being counted falsehood, shall, as I express it,
Be so receiv'd. But thus, if pow'rs divine
Behold our human actions, as they do,
I doubt not then but innocence shall make
False accusation blush, and tyranny
Tremble at patience. You, my lord, best know,
Who least will seem to do so, my past life
Hath been as continent, as chaste, as true,
As I am now unhappy; which is more
Than history can pattern, though devised
And play'd to take spectators. For behold me
A fellow of the royal bed, which owe
A moiety to the throne, a great kings daughter
The mother to a hopeful prince, here standing

To prate and talk for life and honour 'fore
Who please to come and hear. For life, I prize it
As I weigh grief, which I could spare: for honour,
'Tis a derivative from me to mine,
And only that I stand for. I appeal
To your own conscience, sir, before Polixenes
Came to your court, how I was in your grace,
How merited to be so; since he came,
With that encounter so uncurrent I
Have strain'd t' appear thus: if one jot beyond
The bound of honour, or in act or will
That way inclining, harden'd be the hearts
Of all that hear me, and my near'st of kin
Cry fie upon my grave!

The Tragedy of Jane Shore, Nicolas Rowe

Act V, i. Unaware that she has been betrayed by her friend Alicia, Jane Shore speaks before Alicia's door, addressing her transgressions, the diminution of her feelings of malice and revenge.

JANE SHORE

(She enters. Her hair is hanging loose. She is barefoot.)

Yet, yet endure, nor murmur, O my soul!

For are not thy transgressions great and numberless?

Do they not cover thee, like rising floods,

And press thee like a weight of waters down?

Does not the hand of righteousness afflict thee;

And who shall plead against it? Who shall say

To pow'r almighty: "Thou hast done enough:"

Or bid his dreadful rod of vengeance stay?

Wait then with patience till the circling hours

Shall bring the time of thy appointed rest

And lay thee down in death. The hireling thus

With labor drudges out the painful day,

And often looks with long expecting eyes

To see the shadows rise and be dismiss'd.

And hark! methinks the roar that late pursu'd me

Sinks like the murmurs of a falling wind,

And softens into silence. Does revenge

And malice then grow weary, and forsake me?

My guard, too, that observ'd me still so close,

Tire in the task of their inhuman office,
And loiter far behind. Alas! I faint,
My spirits fail at once.—This is the door
Of my Alicia—bless'd opportunity!
I'll steal a little succour from her goodness
Now, while no eye observes me.

   (*She knocks on the door.*)

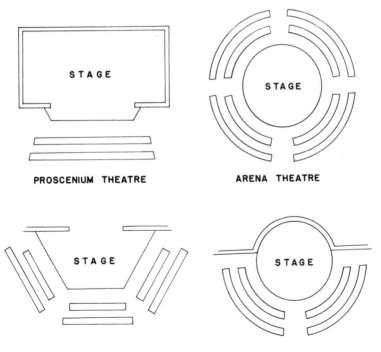

PROSCENIUM THEATRE   ARENA THEATRE

TYPES OF OPEN STAGES

All for Love; or, The World Well Lost, John Dryden

Act III, i. In the following speeches, Octavia, wife of Mark Antony, uses her womanly guile in an attempt to recapture his affections, hoping he will return to her and give up Cleopatra. She has come to Alexandria with their children and uses them, and a promise to set him free without encumbrance as a means of holding him through contrition.

OCTAVIA (FIRST SPEECH)

My hard fortune

Subjects me still to your unkind mistakes.

But the conditions I have brought are such,

You need not blush to take: I love your honour,

Because 'tis mine; it never shall be said,

Octavia's husband was her brother's slave.

Sir, you are free; free, even from her you loathe;

For, though my brother bargains for your love,

Makes me the price and cement of your peace,

I have a soul like yours; I cannot take

Your love as alms, nor beg what I deserve.

I'll tell my brother we are reconciled;

He shall draw back his troops, and you shall march

To rule the East: I may be dropt at Athens;

No matter where. I never will complain,

But only keep the barren name of wife,

And rid you of the trouble.

(SECOND SPEECH)

Sweet Heaven compose it!

Come, come, my Lord, if I can pardon you,

Methinks you should accept it. Look on these;

Are they not yours? or stand they thus neglected,

As they are mine? Go to him, children, go;

Kneel to him, take him by the hand, speak to him;

For you may speak, and he may own you too,

Without a blush; and so he cannot all

His children: go, I say, and pull him to me,

And pull him to yourselves, from that bad woman.

You, Agrippina, hang upon his arms;

And you, Antonia, clasp about his waist:

If he will shake you off, if he will dash you

Against the pavement, you must bear it, children;

For you are mine, and I was born to suffer.

Romeo and Juliet, William Shakespeare

Act III, ii. Juliet, impatiently awaiting Romeo in the Capulet's orchard, pleads for the hastening of night and his arrival, and reveals the deepness of her passion for her lover.

JULIET

Gallop apace, you fiery-footed steeds,

Towards Phoebus' lodging! Such a waggoner

As Phaeton would whip you to the west

And bring in cloudy night immediately.

Spread to close curtain, love-performing night,

That runaways' eyes may wink, and Romeo

Leap to these arms untalked of and unseen.

Lovers can see to do their amorous rites,

By their own beauties; or, if love be blind,

It best agrees with night. Come, civil night,

Thou sober-suited matron, all in black,

And learn me how to lose a winning match,

Played for a pair of stainless maidenhoods:

Hood my unmanned blood, bating in my cheeks

With thy black mantle, till strange love grown bold

Think true love acted simple modesty.

Come, night; come, Romeo; come, thou day in night;

For thou wilt lie upon the wings of night

Whiter than new snow upon a raven's back.

Come, gentle night; come, loving, black-browed night;

Give me my Romeo; and, when he shall die,

Take him and cut him out in little stars,
And he will make the face of heaven so fine
That all the world will be in love with night,
And pay no worship to the garish sun.
O, I have bought the mansion of a love,
But not possessed it; and, though I am sold,
Not yet enjoyed. So tedious is this day
As is the night before some festival
To an impatient child that hath new robes
And may not wear them . . .

Macbeth, William Shakespeare

Act I. Scene v. In a letter to Lady Macbeth, her husband tells of the witches, prophecies of his greatness. Lady Macbeth doubts, however, his ability to carry out the dastardly deeds which will propel him to greatness and correctly realizes that her urging will be necessary if these ends are to be realized.

LADY MACBETH

(Reading.)

"They met me in the day of success; and I have learned by the perfect'st report, they have more in them than mortal knowledge. When I burned in desire to question them further, they made themselves air, into which they vanished. Whiles I stood rapt in the wonder of it, came missives from the King, who all-hailed me 'Thane of Cawdor;' by which title, before, these weird sisters saluted me, and referred me to the coming on of time, with 'Hail, king that shalt be!' This have I thought good to deliver thee, my dearest partner of greatness, that thou mightst not lose the dues of rejoicing, by being ignorant of what greatness is promised thee. Lay it to thy heart, and farewell."

Glamis thou art, and Cawdor, and shalt be
What thou art promised. Yet do I fear thy nature;
It is too full o' the milk of human kindness
To catch the nearest way. Thou wouldst be great;
Art not without ambition, but without
The illness should attend it: what thou wouldst highly,

That wouldst thou holily; wouldst not play false,
And yet wouldst wrongly win; thou'ldst have, great Glamis,
That which cries 'Thus thou must do if you have it;
And that which rather thou dost fear to do
Than wishest should be undone.' Hie thee hither,
That I may pour my spirits in thine ear,
And chastise with the valor of my tongue
All that impedes thee from the golden round,
Which fate and metaphysical aid doth seem
To have thee crowned withal.

Dido, Queen of Carthage, Christopher Marlowe

Act IV, iv. The imminent departure of Aeneas from Carthage has induced great angst in Dido who speaks of ways of detaining him without incurring his disfavor.

DIDO

Speaks not Aeneas like a conqueror?
O blessed tempests that did drive him in!
O happy sand that made him run aground!
Henceforth you shall be our Carthage gods.
Ay, but it may be he will leave my love,
And seek a foreign land call'd Italy.
O that I had a charm to keep the winds
Within the closure of a golden ball;
Or that the Tyrrhene sea were in mine arms,
That he might suffer shipwrack on my breast
As oft as he attempts to hoist up sail!
I must prevent him; wishing will not serve.—
Go bid my nurse take young Ascanius,
And bear him in the country to her house;
Aeneas will not go without his son.
Yet, lest he should, for I am full of fear,
Bring me his oars, his tackling, and his sails.
What if I sink his ships? O, he'll frown!
Better he frown than I should die for grief.
I cannot see him frown; it may not be.

Armies of foes resolv'd to win this town,
Or impious traitors vow'd to have my life,
Affright me not; only Aeneas' frown
Is that which terrifies poor Dido's heart.
Not bloody spears, appearing in the air,
Presage the downfall of my empery,
Nor blazing comets threatens Dido's death;
It is Aeneas' frown that ends my days.
If he forsake me not, I never die,
For in his looks I see eternity,
And he'll make me immortal with a kiss.

Dido, Queen of Carthage, Christopher Marlowe

Act V, i. After Aeneas has departed for Italy, Dido curses him as she burns his belongings. She ends her speech by throwing herself into the flames.

DIDO

Now Dido, with these relics burn thyself,

And make Aeneas famous through the world

For perjury and slaughter of a queen.

Here lie the sword that in the darksome cave

He drew, and swore by, to be true to me.

Thou shalt burn first; thy crime is worse than his.

Here lie the garment which I cloth'd him in

When first he came on shore: perish thou too.

These letters, lines, and perjur'd papers all

Shall burn to cinders in this precious flame.

And now, ye gods, that guide the starry frame,

And order all things at your high dispose,

Grant, though the traitors land in Italy,

They may be still tormented with unrest;

And from mine ashes let a conqueror rise,

That may revenge this treason to a queen

By ploughing up his country with the sword!

Betwixt this land and that be never league;

Live, false Aeneas! Truest Dido dies. . . .

King Richard III, William Shakespeare

Act I, ii. Accompanying the corpse of King Henry to its interment at Chertsey, Anne rails against those who murdered him and her husband, Prince Edward.

ANNE NEVILLE

Set down, set down your honourable load—

If honour may be shrouded in a hearse—

Whilst I awhile obsequiously lament

The untimely fall of virtuous Lancaster.

    (The bearers set down the coffin.)

Poor key-cold figure of a holy king,

Pale ashes of the house of Lancaster,

Thou bloodless remnant of that royal blood,

Be it lawful that I invocate thy ghost

To hear the lamentations of poor Anne,

Wife to thy Edward, to thy slaughtered son,

Stabb'd by the selfsame hand that made these wounds!

Lo, in these windows that let forth thy life

I pour the helpless balm of my poor eyes.

Cursed be the hand that made these holes!

Cursed be the heart that had the heart to do it!

Cursed the blood that let this blood from hence!

More direful hap betide that hated wretch

That makes us wretched by the death of thee

Than I can wish to wolves, to spiders, toads,

Or any creeping venom'd thing that lives!

If ever he have child, abortive be it,
Prodigious, and untimely brought to light,
Whose ugly and unnatural aspect
May fright the hopeful mother at the view;
And that be heir to his unhappiness!
If ever he have wife, let her be made
As miserable by death of him
As I am made by my poor lord and thee!
Come, now towards Chertsey with your holy load,
Taken from Paul's to be interred there;
And still as you are weary of this weight,
Rest you whiles I lament King Henry's corse.

MEN/COMIC

The Merry Wives of Windsor, William Shakespeare

Act II, ii. Mrs. Ford is denying her husband conjugal rights on the grounds of chastity. As a means of overcoming this dilemma, Ford disguises himself and offers to pay Falstaff to seduce Mrs. Ford so that she may not longer claim virginity as a reason for sexual resistance. When the disguised Ford discovers that Falstaff has already had his way with the lady he rages against her deceit and vows hasty revenge.

FORD

What a damn'd Epicurian rascal is this! My heart is ready to crack with impatience. Who says this is improvident jealousy? My wife hath sent to him; the hour is fix'd, the match is made. Would any man have thought this? See the hell of having a false woman! My bed shall be abus'd, my coffers ransack'd, my reputation gnawn at; and I shall not only receive this villanous wrong, but stand under the adoption of abominable terms, and by him that does me this wrong. Terms! Names! Amaimon sounds well; Lucifer, well; Barbason, well; yet they are devils' additions, the names of fiends. But Cuckold! Wittol! Cuckold! the devil himself hath not such a name. Page is an ass, a secure ass. He will trust his wife; he will not be jealous. I will rather trust a Fleming with my butter, Parson Hugh the Welshman with my cheese, an Irishman with my aqua-vitae bottle, or a thief to walk my ambling gelding, than my wife with herself.

Then she plots, then she ruminates, then she devises; and what they think in their hearts they may effect, they will break their hearts but they will effect. God be prais'd for my jealousy! Eleven o'clock the hour. I will prevent this, detect my wife, be revenged on Falstaff, and laugh at Page. I will about it; better three hours too soon than a minute too late. Fie, fie, fie! Cuckold, cuckold, cuckold!

As You Like It, William Shakespeare

Act II, vii. Jaques discourses on his encounter with a fool.

JAQUES

A fool, a fool! I met a fool i' the forest,
A motley fool!—a miserable world!—
As I do live by food, I met a fool.
Who laid him down and bask'd him in the sun,
And rail'd on Lady Fortune in good terms,
In good set terms, and yet a motley fool.
"Good morrow, fool," quoth I. "No sir," quoth he,
"Call me not fool till heaven hath sent me fortune."
And then he drew a dial from his poke,
And, looking on it with lack-lustre eye,
Says very wisely, "It is ten o'clock:
Thus we may see," quoth he, "how the world wags:
'Tis but an hour ago since it was nine,
And after one hour more 'twill be eleven;
And so, from hour to hour, we ripe and ripe;
And then, from hour to hour, we rot and rot;
And thereby hangs a tale." When I did hear
The motley fool thus moral on the time,
My lungs began to crow like a chanticleer,
That fools should be so deep-contemplative,
And I did laugh sans intermission
An hour by his dial.—O noble fool!
A worthy fool! Motley's the only wear.

As You Like It, William Shakespeare

Act II, vii. Jaques, a lord attending the banished Duke, speaks of the seven ages of man.

JAQUES

All the world's a stage,

And all the men and women merely players;

They have their exits and their entrances;

And one man in his time plays many parts,

His acts being seven ages. At the first the infant,

Mewling and puking in the nurse's arms.

Then the whining school-boy, with his satchel

And shining morning face, creeping like snail

Unwillingly to school. And then the lover,

Sighing like furnace, with a woeful ballad

Made to his mistress' eyebrow. Then a soldier,

Full of strange oaths and bearded like the pard,

Jealous in honour, sudden and quick in quarrel,

Seeking the bubble reputation

Even in the cannon's mouth. And then the justice

In fair round belly with good capon lin'd,

With eyes severe and beard of formal cut,

Full of wise saws and modern instances;

And so he plays his part. The sixth age shifts

Into the lean and slipper'd pantaloon,

With spectacles on nose and pouch on side,

His youthful hose well sav'd, a world wide
For his shrunk shank; and his big manly voice,
Turning again toward childish treble, pipes
And whistles in his sound. Last scene of all,
That ends this strange eventful history,
Is second childishness and mere oblivion,
Sans teeth, sans eyes, sans taste, sans every thing.

Epicoene; or, The Silent Woman, Ben Jonson

Act II, ii. Truewit forewarns the gentleman Morose of the pitfalls of marriage.

TRUEWIT

Alas, sir, I am but a messenger: I but tell you, what you must hear. It seems your friends are careful after your soul's health, sir, and would have you know the danger: (but you may do your pleasure for all them, I persuade not, sir). If, after you are married, your wife do run away with a vaulter, or the Frenchman that walks upon ropes, or him that dances the jig, or a fencer for his skill at his weapon; why, it is not their fault, they have discharged their consciences, when you know what may happen. Nay, suffer valiantly, sir, for I must tell you all the perils that you are obnoxious to. If she be fair, young, and vegetous, no sweetmeats ever drew more flies; all the yellow doublets and great roses i' the town will be there. If foul and crooked, she'll be with them, and buy those doublets and roses, sir. If rich, and that you marry her dowry, not her, she'll reign in your house, as imperious as a widow. If noble, all her kindred will be your tyrants. If fruitful, as proud as May, and humorous as April; she must have her doctors, her midwives, her nurses, her longings every hour; though it be for the dearest morsel of man. If learned, there was never such a parrot; all your patrimony will be too little for the guests that must be invited to hear her speak Latin and Greek; and you must lie with her in those languages too, if you will please her. If precise, you must feast all the silenced brethren, once in three days; salute the sisters; entertain the whole family, or wood of 'em; and hear long-winded exercises, singings, and catechizings, which you are not given to, and yet must give for: to please the zealous matron your wife, who for the holy cause, will cozen you, over and above. You begin to sweat, sir! But this is not half, i' faith: you my do your pleasure, notwithstanding, as I said before: I come not to persuade you.

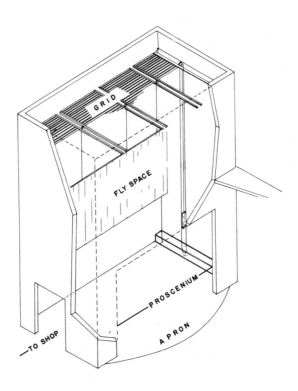

The Jew of Malta, Christopher Marlowe

Act I, i. Barabas, the Jewish miser, is in his counting house with his heaps of gold, reveals his true character.

BARABAS

So that of thus much that return was made;

And of the third part of the Persian ships

There was the venture summ'd and satisfied.

And for those Samnites, and the men of Uz,

That bought my Spanish oils and wines of Greece,

Here have I purs'd their paltry silverlings.

Fie, what trouble 'tis to count this trash!

Well fare the Arabians, who so richly pay

The things they traffic for with wedge of gold,

Whereof a man may easily in a day

Tell that which may maintain him all his life.

The needy groom that never finger'd groat,

Would make a miracle of thus much coin;

But he whose steel-barr'd coffers are cramm'd full,

And all his life-time hath been tired,

Wearying his fingers' ends with telling it,

Would in his age be loath to labour so,

And for a pound to sweat himself to death.

Give me the merchants of the Indian mines,

That trade in metal of the purest mould;

The wealthy Moor, that in the eastern rocks

Without control can pick his riches up,

And in this house heap pearl like pebble stones,

Receive them free, and sell them by the weight!

Bags of fiery opals, sapphires, amethysts,

Jacinths, hard topaz, grass-green emeralds,

Beauteous rubies, sparkling diamonds,

And seld-seen costly stones of so great price,

As one of them indifferently rated,

And of a carat of this quantity,

May serve in peril of calamity,

To ransom great kings from captivity.

This is the ware wherein consists my wealth;

And thus methinks should men of judgement frame

Their means of traffic from the vulgar trade,

And as their wealth increaseth, so inclose

Infinite riches in a little room.

But how now stands the wind?

Into what corner peers my halcyon's bill?

Ha! to the east? Yes. See how stands the vanes?

East and by south: why then I hope my ships

I sent for Egypt and the bordering isles

Are gotten up by Nilus' winding banks;

Mine argosy from Alexandria,

Loaden with spice and silks, now under the sail,

Are smoothly gliding down by Candy-shore

To Malta, through our Mediterranean Sea. . . .

The Jew of Malta, Christopher Marlowe

Act II, iii. Here Barabas relates to Ithamore, a Turkish slave, the many ways by which he has profited through commerce, a practice that has resulted in the acquisition of great wealth.

BARABAS

As for myself, I walk abroad a-nights,

And kill sick people groaning under walls;

Sometimes I go about and poison wells;

And now and then, to cherish Christian thieves,

I am content to lose some of my crowns,

That I may, walking in my gallery,

See 'em go pinion'd along by my door.

Being young, I studied physic, and began

To practice first upon the Italian;

There I enrich'd the priests with burials,

And always kept the sexton's arms in ure

With digging graves and ringing dead men's knells.

And after that, I was an engineer,

And in the wars, 'twixt France and Germany,

Under the pretence of helping Charles the Fifth,

Slew friend and enemy with my stratagems.

Then after I was an usurer,

And with extorting, cozening, forfeiting,

And tricks belonging unto brokery,

I fill'd the gaols with the bankrupts in a year,

And with young orphans planted hospitals,

And every moon made some other mad,
And now and then one hang himself for grief,
Pinning upon his breast a long great scroll
How I with interest tormented him.
But mark how I am blest for plaguing them:
I have as much coin as will by the town. . . .

The Alchemist, Ben Jonson

Act II, iii. Subtle, involved in Alchemy fraud, deftly "explains" the wonders and science of the art to a pair of dupes.

SUBTLE

It is, on the one part,
A humid exhalation, which we call
Materia liquida, or the unctuous water;
On the other part, a certain crass and viscous
Portion of earth; both which, concorporate,
Do make the elementary matter of gold:
Which is not, yet, *propria materia*,
But common to all metals and all stones.
For, where it is forsaken of that moisture,
And hath more dryness, it becomes a stone:
Where it retains more of the humid fatness,
It turns to sulphur, or to quicksilver:
Who are the parents of all other metals.
Nor can this remote matter suddenly
Progress so from extreme unto extreme,
As to grow gold, and leap o'er all the means.
Nature doth first beget the imperfect; then
Proceeds she to the perfect. Of that airy
And oily water, mercury is engendered;
Sulphur o' the fat and earthy part; the one
Which is the last, supplying the place of male,

The other, of the female, in all metals.
Some do believe hermaphrodeity,
That both do act and suffer. But these two
Make the rest ductile, malleable, extensive.
And even in gold they are; for we do find
Seeds in them by our fire, and gold in them:
And can produce the species of each metal
More perfect thence, than nature doth in earth.
Beside, we doth not see in daily practice,
Art can beget bees, hornets, beetles, wasps,
Out of the carcasses and dung of creatures;
Yea, scorpions, of an herb, being rightly placed:
And these are living creatures, far more perfect
And excellent than metals.

The Way of the World, William Congreve

Act IV, i. Mirabell lays down marital conditions to Mrs. Millamant.

MIRABELL

I thank you.—*Imprimis* then, I covenant, that your acquaintance be general; that you admit no sworn confidante, or intimate of your own sex—no she-friend to screen her affairs under your countenance, and tempt you to make trial of a mutual secrecy. No decoy-duck to wheedle you—a fop scrambling to the play in a mask—then bring you home in a pretended fright, when you think you shall be found out—and rail at me for missing the play and disappointing the frolic which you had to pick me up and prove my constancy.

Item, I article, that you continue to like your own face, as long as I shall; and while it passes current with me, that you endeavor not to new-coin it. To which end, together with all vizards of the day, I prohibit all masks for the night, made of oiled-skins, and I know not what—hogs' bones, hares' gall, pig-water, and the marrow of a roasted cat. In short, I forbid all commerce with the gentlewoman in what-d'ye-call-it court. *Item,* I shut my doors against all bawds with baskets, and pennyworths of muslin, china, fans, atlases, etc. *Item,* when you shall be breeding—Which may be presumed a blessing on our endeavors—

I denounce against all strait lacing, squeezing for a shape, till you mold my boy's head like a sugarloaf, and instead of a man-child, make me father to a crooked billet. Lastly, to the dominion of the tea-table I submit —but with proviso, that you exceed not in your province; but restrain yourself to native and simple tea-table drinks, as tea, chocolate, and coffee: as likewise to genuine and authorized tea-table talk—such as mending of fashions, spoiling reputations, railing at absent friends, and so forth—but that on no account you encroach upon the men's prerogative, and presume to drink healths, or toast fellows; for prevention of which I banish all foreign forces, all auxiliaries to the tea-table, as orange-brandy, all aniseed, cinnamon, citron, and Barbadoes waters, together with ratafia, and the most noble spirit of clary, but for cowslip wine, poppy water, and all dormitives, those I allow.—These provisos admitted, in other things I may prove a tractable and complying husband.

MEN/DRAMATIC

Macbeth, William Shakespeare

*Act II, i. Stirred by the witches prophecies and goaded by Lady
Macbeth, Macbeth contemplates his evil deed and awaits the
signal that will dispatch him to the murder of Duncan.*

MACBETH

Is this a dagger which I see before me,

The handle toward my hand? Come, let me clutch thee!

I have thee not, and yet I see thee still.

Art thou not, fatal vision, sensible

To feeling as to sight? Or art thou but

A dagger of the mind, a false creation,

Proceeding from the heat-oppressed brain?

I see thee yet, in form as palpable

As this which now I draw.

Thou marshall'st me the way I was going;

And such an instrument I was to use.

Mine eyes are made the fools o' the other senses,

Or else worth all the rest. I see thee still;

And on thy blade and dudgeon gouts of blood,

Which was not so before. There's no such thing:

It is the bloody business which informs

Thus to mine eyes. Now o'er the one half-world

Nature seems dead, and wicked dreams abuse

The curtained sleep. Witchcraft celebrates

Pale Hecate's offerings; and withered murder,
Alarumed by his sentinel, the wolf,
Whose howl's his watch, thus with his stealthy pace,
With Tarquin's ravishing strides, towards his design
Moves like a ghost. Thou sure and firm-set earth,
Hear not my steps, which way they walk, for fear
Thy very stones prate of my whereabout,
And take the present horror from the time,
Which now suits with it. Whiles I threat, he lives:
Words to the heat of deeds to cold breath gives.

    (*A bell sounds.*)

I go, and it is done: the bell invites me.
Hear it not, Duncan, for it is a knell
That summons thee to heaven or to hell.

Edward the Second, Christopher Marlowe

Act III, ii. Edward's words reveal the wrath he possesses for those who are plotting against him.

EDWARD

(Kneels and speaks.)

By earth, the common mother of us all,

By Heaven, and all the moving orbs thereof,

By this right hand, and by my father's sword,

And all the honours 'longing to my crown,

I will have heads and lives for him, as many

As I have manors, castles, towns, and towers.

Treacherous Warwick! Traitorous Mortimer!

If I be England's king, in lakes of gore

Your headless trunks, your bodies will I trail,

That you may drink your fill, and quaff in blood,

And stain my royal standard with the same;

That so my bloody colours may suggest

Remembrance of revenge immortally

On your accursed traitorous progeny,

You villains that have slain my Gaveston.

And in this place of honour and of trust,

Spencer, sweet Spencer, I adopt thee here,

And merely of our love we do create thee

Earl of Gloucester and Lord Chamberlain,

Despite of times, despite of enemies.

Edward the Second, Christopher Marlowe

*Act V, i. In the presence of the Bishop of Winchester and Earl
of Leicester, Edward rails against his traitors, explaining that
revenge is a ruler's prerogative lest his powers be vitiated.*

EDWARD

Leicester, if gentle words might comfort me,

They speeches long ago had eas'd my sorrows;

For kind and loving hast thou always been.

The griefs of private men are soon allay'd,

But not of kings: the forest deer being struck,

Runs to an herb that closeth up the wounds,

But when the imperial lion's flesh is gor'd

He rends and tears it with his wrathful paw,

And highly scorning that the lowly earth

Should drink his blood, mounts up into the air.

And so it fares with me, whose dauntless mind

The ambitious Mortimer would seek to curb,

And that unnatural queen, false Isabel,

That thus has pent and mew'd me in a prison;

For such outrageous passions cloy my soul,

As with the wings of rancor and disdain,

Full often I am soaring up to Heaven,

To plain me to the gods against them both.

But when I call to mind that I am king,

Methinks me should revenge me of my wrongs,

That Mortimer and Isabel have done.

But what are kings, when regiment is gone,
But perfect shadows in a sunshine day?
My nobles rule, I bear the name of king:
I wear the crown; but I am controll'd by them,
By Mortimer and my unconstant queen
Who spots my nuptial bed with infamy;
Whilst I am lodg'd within this cave of care,
Where sorrow at my elbow still attends
To company my heart with sad laments,
That bleeds within me for this strange exchange.
But tell me, must I now resign my crown,
To make usurping Mortimer a king?

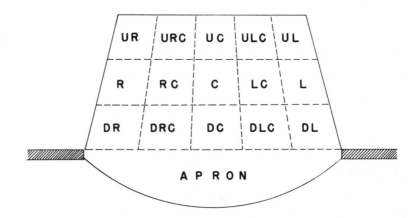

Dido, Queen of Carthage, C. Marlowe

Act II, i. Aeneas recants Troy's fall to his love, Dido.

AENEAS

O, th' enchanting words of that base slave
Made him to think Epeus' pine-tree horse
A sacrifice t' appease Minerva's wrath!
The rather for that one Laocoon,
Breaking a spear upon his hollow breast,
Was with two winged serpents stung to death.
Whereat aghast, we were commanded straight
With reverence to draw it into Troy,
In which unhappy work as I employ'd.
These hands did help to hale it to the gate,
Through which I could not enter, 'twas so huge —
O had it never enter'd, Troy had stood!
But Priamus, impatient of delay,
Enforc'd a wide breach in that rampir'd wall
Which thousand battering-rams could never pierce,
And so came this fatal instrument,
At whose accursed feet, as overjoy'd,
We banqueted, till, overcome with wine,
Some surfeited, and others soundly slept.
Which Sinon viewing, caus'd the Greekish spies
To haste to Tenedos and tell the camp.
Then he unlock'd the horse; and suddenly,

From out his entrails, Neoptolemus,
Setting his spear upon the ground, leapt forth,
And, after him, a thousand Grecians more,
In whose stern faces shin'd the quenchless fire
That after burnt the pride of Asia.
By this the camp was come unto the walls,
And through the breach did march into the streets,
Where, meeting with the rest, "Kill, kill!" they cried.
Frighted with this confused noise, I rose,
And looking from a turret, might behold
Young infants swimming in their parents' blood,
Headless carcasses pil'd up in heaps,
Virgins half-dead dragg'd by their golden hair
And with main force flung on a ring of pikes,
Old men with swords thrust through their aged sides,
Kneeling for mercy to a Greekish lad,
Who with steel poleaxes dash'd out their brains.
Then buckled I mine armour, drew my sword.
And thinking to go down, came Hector's ghost,
With ashy visage, blueish sulphur eyes,
His arms torn from his shoulders, and his breast
Furrow'd with wounds, and, that which made me weep,
Thongs at his heels, by which Achilles' horse
Drew him in triumph through the Greekish camp,
Burst from the earth, crying "Aeneas fly!
Troy is afire, the Grecians have the town!"

Doctor Faustus, Christopher Marlowe

Act V, ii. Faustus decries his fate during his final hour, before his descent to hell.

FAUSTUS

Ah Faustus,

Now hast thou but one bare hour to live,

And then you must be damned perpetually.

Stand still, you ever-moving spheres of heaven,

That time may cease and midnight never come;

Fair nature's eye, rise, rise again, and make

Perpetual day. Or let this hour but be

A year, a month, a week, a natural day,

That Faustus may repent and save his soul.

O lente, lente, currite noctis equi.

The stars move still, time runs, the clock will strike.

The devil will come, and Faustus must be damned.

Oh, I'll leap up to my God: who pulls me down?

See, see, where Christ's blood streams in the firmament.

One drop would save my soul, half a drop. Ah my Christ!

Ah, end not my heart for naming of my Christ;

Yet will I call on him: Oh, spare me Lucifer!

Where is it now? Tis gone:

And see where God stretcheth out his arms

And bends his ireful brows.

Mountains and hills, come, come, and fall on me

And hide me from the heavy wrath of God!
No no: Then will I headlong run into the earth.
Earth gape! O no, it will not harbor me.
You stars the reigned at my nativity,
Whose influence hath allotted death and hell,
Now draw up Faustus like a foggy mist
Into the entrails of yon laboring cloud,
That when you vomit forth into the air,
My limbs may issue from your smoky mouths,
So that my soul may but ascend to heaven.
     (The watch strikes.)
Ah, half the hour is passed,
'Twill all be passed anon.
O God, If thou will not have mercy on my soul,
Yet for Christ's sake, whose blood hath ransomed me,
Impose some end to my incessant pain.
Let Faustus live in hell a thousand years,
A hundred thousand, and at last be saved.
Oh, no end is limited to damned souls.
Why wert thou not a creature wanting soul?
Or why is this immortal that thou hast?
Ah, Pythagoras *metempsychosis* were that true
This soul should fly from me, and I be changed
Unto some brutish beast.
All beasts are happy or when they die
Their souls are soon dissolved in elements,

But mine must live still to be plagued in hell.
Cursed be the parents that engendered me!
No, Faustus, curse thyself, curse Lucifer,
That hath deprived thee of the joys of heaven.
>   (*The clock strikes twelve.*)
It strikes, it strikes! Now body turn to air,
Or Lucifer will bear thee quick to hell.
>   (*Thunder and lightning.*)
Oh soul, be changed into little water drops
And fall into the ocean, ne'er to be found.
>   (*Thunder. Enter the Devils.*)
My God, my God! Look not so fierce on me.
Adders and serpents, let me breathe awhile.
Ugly hell, gape not, come not, Lucifer!
I'll burn my books! Ah, Mephostophilis!

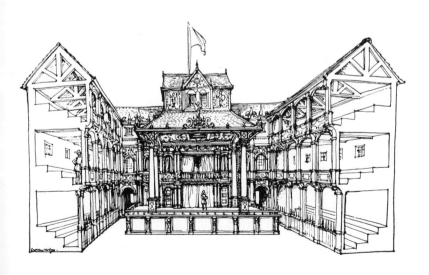

The London Merchant, George Lillo

Act III, v. Here a contrite Barnwell agonizes over being party to an embezzling scheme, his lust, and his plans for murdering his uncle.

BARNWELL

A dismal gloom obscures the face of day; either the sun has slip'd behind a cloud, or journeys down the west of heaven, with more than common speed to avoid the sight of what I'm doom'd to act. Since I set forth on this accursed design, where'er I tread, methinks, the solid earth trembles beneath my feet. Yonder limpid stream, whose hoary fall has made a natural cascade, as I pass'd by, in doleful accents seem'd to murmur "Murder." The earth, the air, the water, seem concern'd—but that's not strange: the world is punish'd, and nature feels the shock, when Providence permits a good man's fall! Just Heaven! Then what should I be! For him, that was my father's only brother, and since his death has been to me a father, who took me up an infant, and an orphan, rear'd me with tenderest care, and still indulged me with most paternal fondness yet here I stand avow'd his destin'd murderer! I stiffen with horror at my own impiety; 'tis yet unperformed. What if I quit my bloody purpose, and fly the place!

(He starts to go, then stops.)

But whither, O whither, shall I fly? My master's once friendly doors are ever shut against me; and without money Millwood will never see me more, and life is not to be endured without her. She's got such firm possession of my heart, and governs there with such despotic sway. Aye, there's the cause of all my sin and sorrow! 'Tis more than love; 'tis the fever of the soul and madness of desire. In vain does nature, reason, conscience, all oppose it; the impetuous passion bears down all before it, and drives me on to lust, to theft, and murder.—Oh conscience! feeble guide to virtue, who only shows us when we go astray, but wants the power to stop us in our course.—Ha, in yonder shady walk I see my uncle. He's alone. Now for my disguise!

(*He takes out a visor.*)

This is his hour of private meditation. Thus daily he prepares his soul for heaven, whilst I—but what have I to do with heaven? —Ha! No struggles, conscience.—

Hence, hence, remorse, and ev'ry thought that's good;
The storm that lust began must end in blood.

(*He dons the visor, draws a pistol, and exits.*)

Othello, William Shakespeare

Act II, iii. The duplicitous Iago contrives to set Othello, the Moor, against his lieutenant Cassio and instill jealousy in him for his wife Desdemona. He instigates a drunken brawl involving Cassio and then summons Othello to investigate. After Othello finds his lieutenant derelict of duties and discharges him, Iago encourages Cassio to ask for Desdemona's help in restoring him to his position of authority and regaining Othello's confidence. Iago's motive here is to make Othello believe that she is pleading Cassio's case out of her love for him.

IAGO

And what's he then that says I play the villain?

When this advice is free I give and honest,

Probal to thinking, and indeed the course

To win the Moor again? For 'tis most easy

Th' inclining Desdemona to subdue

In any honest suit. She's fram'd as fruitful

As the free elements. And then for her

To win the Moor—were't to renounce his baptism—

All seals and symbols of redeemed sin—

His soul is so enfetter'd to her love

That she may make, unmake, do what she list,

Even as her appetite shall play the god

With his weak function. How am I then a villain

To counsel Cassio to this parallel course,

Directly to his good? Divinity of hell!

When devils will the blackest sins put on,
They do suggest at first with heavenly shows,
As I do now. For whiles this honest fool
Plies Desdemona to repair his fortunes,
And she for him pleads strongly to the Moor,
I'll pour this pestilence into his ear—
That she repeals him for her body's lust;
And by how much she strives to do him good.
She shall undo her credit with the Moor.
So I will turn her virtue into pitch,
And out of her own goodness make the net
That shall enmesh them all.

Julius Caesar, William Shakespeare

Act III, i. First, in the presence of Caesar's murderers, Mark Antony feigns understanding and embraces them, appearing to make peace.

ANTONY

I doubt not of your wisdom.

Let each man render me his bloody hand:

First, Marcus Brutus, will I shake with you;

Next, Caius Cassius, do I take your hand;

Now, Decius Brutus, yours; now yours, Metellus;

Yours, Cinna; and, my valiant Casca, yours.

Though last, not least in love, yours, good Trebonius.

Gentlemen all—Alas, what shall I say?

My credit now stands on such slippery ground

That one of two bad ways you must conceit me,

Either a coward or a flatterer.

That I did love thee, Caesar, O, 'tis true!

If then thy spirit look upon us now,

Shall it not grieve thee dearer than thy death,

To see thy Antony making his peace,

Shaking the bloody fingers of thy foes,

Most noble! in the presence of thy corse?

Had I as many eyes as thou hast wounds,

Weeping as fast as they stream forth thy blood,

It would become me better than to close

In terms of friendship with thine enemies.

Pardon me, Julius! Here wast thou bay'd, brave hart;
Here didst thou fall; and here my hunters stand,
Sign'd in thy spoil, and crimson'd in thy lethe.
O world, thou wast the forest to this hart;
And this, indeed, O world, the heart of thee!
How like a deer, strucken by many princes,
Dost thou here lie!

All for Love; or, The World Well Lost, John Dryden

Act III, i. Mark Antony reminds his friend Dolabella that when he first saw Cleopatra he was so taken by the her that he had retracted his accusation that she had murdered his brother.

ANTONY

She lay, and leant her cheek upon her hand,

And cast a look so languishingly sweet

As if, secure of all beholders' hearts,

Neglecting, she could take them: boys like Cupids,

Stood fanning, with their painted wings, the winds

That played about her face. But if she smiled

A darting glory seemed to blaze abroad,

That men's desiring eyes were never wearied,

But hung upon the object: To soft flutes

The silver oars kept time; and while they played,

The hearing gave new pleasure to the sight;

And both to thought. 'Twas heaven, or somewhat more;

For she so charmed all hearts, that gazing crowds

Stood panting on the shore, and wanted breath

To give their welcome voice.

Then, Dolabella, where was then thy soul?

Was not thy fury quite disarmed with wonder?

Didst thou not shrink behind me with those eyes

And whisper in my ear—"Oh, tell her not

That I accused her of my brother's death?"